YOUNG ENGINEERS

Building Vehicles that Roll

by Tammy Enz

capstone

© 2017 Heinemann-Raintree
an imprint of Capstone Global Library, LLC
Chicago, Illinois

To contact Capstone Global Library please call 800-747-4992, or visit our website www.mycapstone.com

Edited by Adrian Vigliano
Designed by Philippa Jenkins
Picture research by Svetlana Zhurkin
Production by Katy LaVigne
Originated by Capstone Global Library Ltd

21 20 19 18 17
10 9 8 7 6 5 4 3

Library of Congress Cataloging-in-Publication Data
Library of Congress Cataloging-in-Publication data is available on the Library of Congress website.

ISBN: 9781484637487 (library binding)
ISBN: 9781484637524 (pbk.)

Acknowledgments
The author and publisher are grateful to the following for permission to reproduce copyright material:
Capstone Studio: Karon Dubke, cover, 8, 9, 12, 13, 16, 17, 20, 21, 22, 23, 26, 27; Dreamstime: Ruslan Kudrin, 5; Shutterstock: Adrian C, 19, Anirut Thailand, 29, Dan74, 15, Evgeny Murtola, 25, javarman, 7, Thor Jorgen Udvang, 11

We would like to thank Harold Pratt for his help in the preparation of this book.

Every effort has been made to contact copyright holders of any material reproduced in this book. Any omissions will be rectified in subsequent printings if notice is given to the publisher.

Printed in the United States of America.
052017   010535RP

Table of Contents

Some words are shown in bold, **like this.** You can find out what they mean by looking in the glossary.

Get Rolling

You depend on your bicycle or your family's car to get you moving. But you also need a comfortable and safe ride. Vehicles can run on gas, electricity, or pedal **power**. But there's more to a vehicle than power. Designing ways to get power to the wheels and ways to stop vehicles keeps engineers busy. They also design ways to keep passengers safe in a crash.

Engineers think about safety and fun when designing cars.

Engine and Transmission

The amount of power a vehicle needs depends on how fast it needs to travel. It also depends on the weight of the vehicle. Vehicles that don't weigh much need less power to travel faster. A person can pedal hard enough to power a lightweight bike. But heavy trucks need powerful **diesel** engines to get going.

The heavier a vehicle is, the more power it needs to get moving.

7

Build a Car

In this experiment, you can build a model car. After you've built it, load up your new vehicle to see how extra weight affects its performance.

You will need:

- 4 plastic milk jug caps
- 2 wooden skewers
- A 6 inch (15 centimeter) square of corrugated cardboard
- A coffee mug

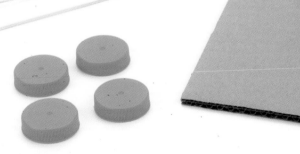

1. Poke a hole in the center of each cap with a pointed skewer end.

2. Stick the skewers through openings at opposite ends of the cardboard.

3. Slide caps onto the skewer ends to make wheels. Make sure the wheels can move freely. Push the car across a smooth floor.

4. Set the mug on the car. Is it harder to push? Now place heavy objects such as metal silverware inside the mug. How is the car affected as weight is added?

A **transmission** moves power from a car's engine to its wheels. A transmission is a set of **gears** that can change the speed or **reverse** the direction of an engine's power. Car engines are powerful. When a car needs to travel slower, its power needs to be reduced. Toothed gears can do that. You'll find toothed gears on your bike too. Bike gears transfer pedal power to spinning wheels.

Toothed gears are useful in many different types of machines.

Make Some Gears

See how gears transfer power with this experiment.

You will need:

- Two plastic lids (different sizes)
- About 16 push pins (all one color)
- 2 push pins (different color)
- Cardboard box

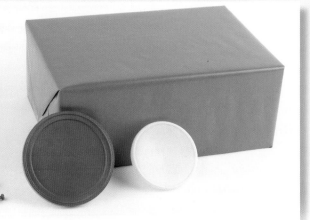

1. Press pins evenly along the rims of each lid about 1 inch (2.5 cm) apart. Use one different colored pin on each lid.

2. Turn the box upside down and pin the lid centers to its bottom. The gears should slightly overlap with the different colored pins touching.
3. Slowly spin one of the gears. What happens to the different colored pins?
4. Change the direction of the spinning gear. What happens to the two differently colored pins now?

Drag

Cars need powerful engines to move their massive weight. But cars use most of their engine power to fight **drag**. Drag is the force caused by air when an object tries to push past it. The faster a car goes the more drag works against it. Drag affects sleek, rounded cars, like race cars, less than boxy cars. Every surface of a sleek race car is designed to reduce drag and let air flow smoothly over the body.

Engineers make cars as smooth as possible to reduce drag.

Experiment with Drag

You can see how an object's shape affects drag with this experiment.

You will need:

- 2 empty closed cardboard cereal boxes
- A hair dryer

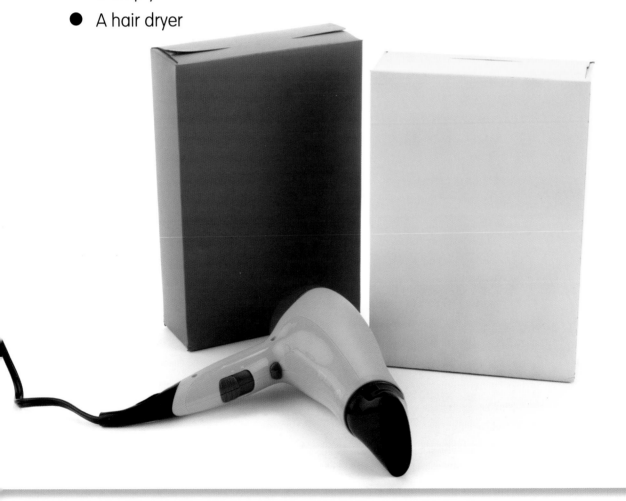

1. Lay one box on its face.
2. Hold the hair dryer about 6 inches (15 cm) away and blow on the side of the box. What happens?
3. Set the other box on its side.
4. Hold the hair dryer about 6 inches (15 cm) away and blow on its face. Which box is affected more by the force of blowing air?

Tires and Brakes

Rubber tires help give you a comfortable ride. But rubber tires are important for another reason. Rubber grips the road and keeps cars from sliding. This grip is called **friction**. Friction is especially important when vehicles turn corners and stop quickly. Brakes use friction too. Brakes squeeze a car's wheels, allowing friction to stop the vehicle.

The patterns on tires are designed to help grip the road surface.

Experiment with Tires

See how friction keeps a wheel from skidding in this experiment.

You will need:

- A plastic jar lid
- A rubber band slightly smaller than the lid

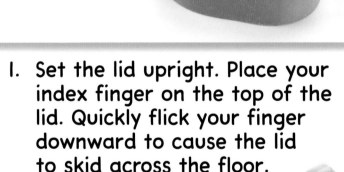

1. Set the lid upright. Place your index finger on the top of the lid. Quickly flick your finger downward to cause the lid to skid across the floor.

2. Now wrap the rubber band around the lid.

3. Repeat step 1. Are you able to make the rubber covered lid skid?

Making Brakes

See how brakes use friction to stop cars in this experiment.

You will need:
- A pencil
- An old CD or DVD

1. Slide the pencil through the hole in the CD.
2. Hold the pencil horizontally.

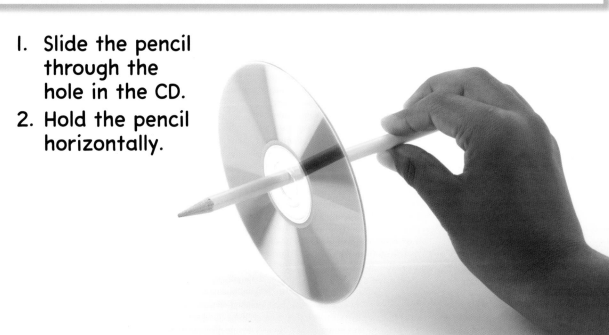

3. With your other hand begin spinning the CD around the pencil like a rolling wheel.

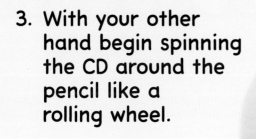

4. Now quickly pinch the edge of the CD with your fingers. Does the friction from your fingers stop the CD?

Bumpers

A bumper has an important job.
It protects a car and the people
inside if the car bumps into something
at low speed. Bumpers are made to
be crushed when they hit something.
They help **absorb** the force of a
crash to protect important parts of
the car. They are often made from
a plastic shell with a softer crushable
material beneath.

Sometimes a car's bumper cannot absorb all of the force of a crash.

Experiment with Bumpers

See how bumpers work in this experiment.

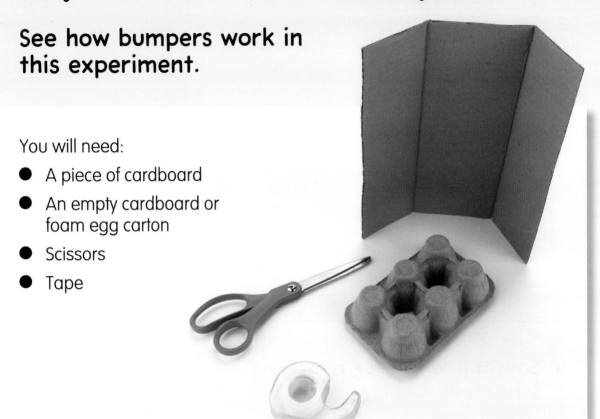

You will need:

- A piece of cardboard
- An empty cardboard or foam egg carton
- Scissors
- Tape

1. Cut a piece of cardboard about the size of the egg carton section. Bend its ends so it sits upright with enough room to slide the carton under it.

2. Tape the ends of the cardboard to a table.
3. Test the cardboard bumper by smashing it with your fist.

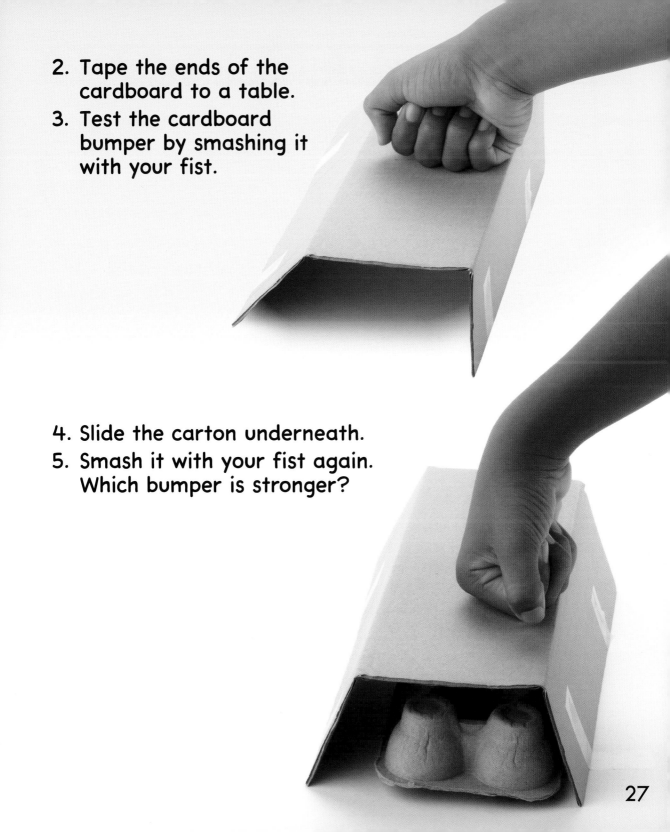

4. Slide the carton underneath.
5. Smash it with your fist again. Which bumper is stronger?

Wheeled vehicles make traveling fast and fun. But they need lots of parts to get going, slow down, and stay safe. Next time you are outside, take a look at the vehicles around you. Think about what's powering each one. What are their gears used for? Which parts help drivers stop and keep passengers safe?

Engineers work hard each day to design the next great car.

Glossary

absorb—to take up

diesel—fuel for trucks

drag—slowing force caused by air

friction—slowing force caused by objects rubbing together

gears—toothed wheels

power—energy source

reverse—to go the other way

transmission—something that moves power to wheels

Find Out More

Books

Dinmont, Kerry. *Motorcycles on the Go*. Machines That Go. Minneapolis: Lerner Publications, 2017.

Gray, Leon. *Fast and Cool Cars*. DK Adventures. New York: DK, Penguin Random House, 2015.

Kenney, Karen Latchana. *Thrilling Sports Cars*. Dream Cars. North Mankato, Minn.: Capstone Press, 2015.

Internet sites

Facthound offers a safe, fun way to find Internet sites related to this book. All of the sites on Facthound have been researched by our staff.

Here's all you do:
Visit *www.facthound.com*
Type in this code: 9781484637487

Index